MW00352358

He's Always There for You

A Collection of Inspirational Writings

Irene Bryan

ISBN 978-1-0980-6876-9 (paperback)
ISBN 978-1-0980-6877-6 (digital)

Copyright © 2020 by Irene Bryan

All rights reserved. No part of this publication may be reproduced, distributed, or transmitted in any form or by any means, including photocopying, recording, or other electronic or mechanical methods without the prior written permission of the publisher. For permission requests, solicit the publisher via the address below.

Christian Faith Publishing, Inc.
832 Park Avenue
Meadville, PA 16335
www.christianfaithpublishing.com

Printed in the United States of America

My Soul Rests in Him

Yes, my soul, find rest in God;
my hope comes from him. Truly he is my rock and my
salvation; he is my fortress, I will not be shaken.

—Psalm 62:5–6 NIV

There are situations that will come. Some will be overwhelming and stressful to the soul, some will be a heavy burden on the soul, and some situations will be a time of great pressure upon the soul. In such times in life, God invites that soul to come and rest in Him. Psalm 62:5 reads, "Find rest, O my soul, in the Lord." Rest for the soul is important to the Lord. Yet how many times do we really accept his offer to come and rest? God is there for us. He understands what the soul is in need of, and He is able to supply. God is not only present, He is also a provider to the soul. Whatever the soul is in need of, God can be trusted to provide. Rest is one thing we all need. Those who choose to rest in Him, He is able to renew and restore their souls in such a way that they will rise up like the eagle. Rest is a blessing, and it is good for the soul. God is always with you, and He always knows what you need. And sometimes that need is rest.

Like a mighty eagle, the Lord can elevate, uplift, and rise up the soul of the weary, weak, and wounded; and in Him their souls can find rest. There is rest for the stressed, frustrated, fearful, uncertain, and troubled soul. There is rest to be found for the soul who has the faith to look beyond what is and see what is yet to be. There is rest for the soul who trusts in the Lord; who believes nothing is too hard or impossible for Him to do; who depends and relies on His word, power, and promises; and who recognizes and acknowledges that all of their help comes from Him. There is rest for the soul who takes refuge and shelter in Him in times of trouble. There is rest for the soul of the despaired, depressed, dismayed, and discouraged. There is rest to be had for the soul who seeks shelter, who longs for guidance and directions, and who desperately wants comfort and peace. There is refreshment and rest for all who are willing to come and dwell in Him. There is rest to be found for the soul who casts their burdens on Him, whose focus is steadfast on Him instead of their situations and storms. There is truly refreshment and rest waiting for the soul who is willing to come and dwell in Him, for in Him there is rest for the soul regardless of the situation. Today, if your soul is in need of rest, I pray you will find it in the Lord—I did. May the Lord give you rest in Him.

Footnote: God is always there to provide the soul with whatever it is in need of.

No Matter What, He's There

Never will I leave you; never will I forsake you.

—Hebrews 13:5

No matter what the situation, trouble, or problem is, He is there with and for you. He's there as your refuge and shelter; He is your safety and security. He's your hiding place; your dwelling place to go to for support and strength from life's storms, situations, and troubles. At times in life, there will be some powerful and hard situations to face. Yet nothing you face is ever more powerful than God. God is all-powerful and all-knowing; He is able to work out any situation you face. Do you know that God already has a solution to the situation before it becomes a situation in your life? You just have to wait on His solution with the assurance that He is able to do anything, even though it may look not so. Consider that you are called upon to look by faith and not by sight. When it comes to your life's troubles, Psalm 46:1 reminds you that God is a refuge and an ever-present help in time of trouble. In fact, you can have confidence in spite of your trouble that God is with you, and He is able to help you. He is an ever-present help; unlike man, God will never leave or forsake you in your time of need.

Whatever you face, God also faces. Although life's situations can cause you to become anxious, stressful, and fretful, God is able to give you calmness, quietness, and peace. When it comes to life's situations, it is good to maintain determination, discipline, and endurance so you will be able with God's help to continue to persevere, no matter the circumstances. Although it can be difficult and hard to pertain to these three things, it is possible with God's help and the Holy Spirit. The Holy Spirit is with you as a helper, guide, and comforter. You can be assured and certain that both God and His spirit are with you in whatever you face. Nothing you deal with or encounter in life is a shock or surprise to Him. He is never caught off guard or unprepared for any of your troubles, problems, situations, or circumstances, whether expected or unexpected, because the truth is God knows everything even before it becomes visible in your life. God is all-knowing; He is the God of the visible as well as the invisible. For all things are before Him, therefore nothing comes forth He is ever unaware of, and nothing is too hard or impossible for Him to ever do. He has a solution for every situation. However, it is up to you to believe and trust Him for the solution.

John 2:29 states that "blessed are those who have not seen and yet have believed." Is it always easy to believe before seeing? No, it is not, but it is also possible with God, His word, and the Holy Spirit. All three are powerful, and all three have a great influence and impact on how you face and deal with your various situations and troubles when they come into your life.

Sometimes you can be caught up into some challenging, painful, and difficult situations from the choices of others with and around you. But even in such times you can draw strength from God, wisdom from His word, and direction and guidance from the Holy Spirit. God's grace, mercy, provision, and help are always available to you, whatever your situation in life. Even in your darkest of times, your worst of times, and your painful times, He is able to change it into victory.

Psalm 139:16 scripture reminds you that all the days ordained for you were written in His book before one of them came to be. God had already ordained what would be in your life before it ever came to be. He had already put His seal of approval on the situation to become active. It is God who activates the situation, and it is God who is faithful and trustworthy in times of trouble. There is a season to every situation and a time to end, and God is in control and in charge of both. It would be wonderful if there were never any troubles, trials, problems, pain, hardships, hurts, sorrow, grief, or suffering. But the reality is there will always be. However, the reality and good news to you is whatever will be, God will be there with you ready to meet the need.

Footnote: No matter what trials and troubles you face in life, God is there and will help you to endure.

When the Soul Is in Need

Your word is a lamp to my feet and a light for my path.

—Psalm 119:105

Through his word we learn that God is always there for the soul in need. We learn through his word that He is ever present. Through his word we learn that God is always able and available to help. And through his word we learn to trust him never to leave us to face anything alone. When the soul is in need, God's word is able to supply all we need. This means that God is always there for us. In fact, the Word is the prescription for every need the soul has. When the soul is in need of comfort, peace, and encouragement, it can be found in the Word. Whatever the situation, there is an answer in the Word for the soul who seeks, believes, and trusts. For example, Isaiah 26:3 states that there is peace for the soul whose mind is steadfast on the Lord and trusts in him. Listen to what Isaiah 26:3 says, "You will keep in perfect peace him whose mind is steadfast because he trusts in you." The scripture suggests that peace comes to those whose mind is steadfast on the Lord and who trust in the Lord. Key words are steadfast and trust; and the message is, if one wants to have peace, no matter the situation or what one is going through, it begins and ends with one's decision to stay focused on the Lord and His power instead of the situation. It helps the mind to be at peace for the mind will be on the Lord and the things of the Lord, which, in return, allows the soul to trust in the Lord's ability to solve the issue, whatever it may be.

The Word of God is a mantle book full of instructions to the mind, heart, and soul. It is the vitamins A, B, C, and D for a healthy and productive life. It is the word of the Lord which is the blueprint for building one's life on. It is the word which is able to be a lamp to the path one walks on. It is the word of God which gives direction, guidance, wisdom, and understanding to what is and what is not pleasing to the Lord. Everything one needs to meet one's situation is there in His word, if one is willing to do the following seven things. First, seek after it. Second, apply it. Third, have faith in it. Fourth, believe it. Fifth, trust it. Sixth, obey it. And seventh, depend on it. Each one of these things is necessary to do when one finds one's self looking to His word for a certain need in one's life. For example, if one wants a word of comfort or encouragement, it is there. If the soul longs to have peace, there's a word to offer peace to the soul. However, what one is in need of, one must be willing to seek after it in the Lord, and when it is found, one must apply what is found as well as have faith, belief, and trust in, and also obey and depend on.

The word is life, light, and liberty for the soul. It is the diet for eliminating the weight of heavy burdens, cares, concern, and worry. The word of God is medicine to the mind, heart, and soul. It calms the fearful, strengthens the weak, restores the broken, comforts the sorrowful, refreshes the weary, and encourages the discouraged. Whatever the soul longs for can be discovered in God's word. His word is powerful, helpful, trustful, truthful, and dependable.

When the soul is in need, the word of God shall supply the need, for it will never disappoint the soul that seeks, accepts, believes, trusts, follows, and has faith in Him and His word. Today, if your soul is in need for peace, comfort, or anything else, why not let the Holy Spirit and the word of God help you fulfill the need? May God bless, guide, and lead you in the way you should always go.

Footnote: Whatever your soul needs, God's word is always available to meet that need.

Hold On, Things Will Get Better

And we know that in all things God works
for the good of those who love him, and who have
been called according to his purpose.

—Romans 8:28

At times life brings storms, but deep inside of the storm God is also there, and He has a solution; so hold on, things will get better. At times life brings rainstorms, but in the shadows of the rainstorm, God has a beautiful, colorful rainbow ready to appear. At times life brings problems that are hard to deal with, but to every problem God has a purpose, plan, and provision for it; so hold on, things will get better. At times life brings times of darkness, but beneath the darkness, dawn waits on God's okay to overtake the darkness; so hold on, things will get better. At times life brings gray skies, yet in the midst of the gray is the color blue ready to make its debut; so hold on, things will get better. At times life brings cloudy days, but behind the clouds, the sun is resting until it's time to shine; so hold on, things will get better.

Sometimes one can only see what is, but in every situation, something else is beneath what's already is and the something else is totally different from what is. What is, is the thing that is already happening, and the something else is what is hoped for to happen that is opposite of what already is. What is will only be for a moment because there is something else waiting in the wings, ready to soar above what is. To every situation, regardless of how painful or hurtful the situation, a solution waits in the background to spring forth at the appointed season and proper time set by God; so don't lose hope, because things will get better. Today, if you are going through some storms, dark times, problems, or hardships, be encouraged because things will get better; so hold on, don't lose heart or hope. God is on your side, His grace is sufficient, and He loves you; so hold on, don't give up, because things will get better.

Footnote: When you are facing storms in your life, hold on, because God is with you and He will see you through your storms.

Life's Dark and Dawn Times

To everything there is a season, purpose, and time.

—Ecclesiastes 3:1

Life brings many seasons, and each is designed to serve a purpose. Sometimes life gives us dark times and sometimes it gives us the dawn times. No one enjoys the dark times in life; you know, those times when one storm after the next blows in without any rest in between before another storm happens. Storm after storm continues to come, with each storm being a little more powerful and darker with no letup in sight. If people had a choice between the dark times and the dawn times in their lives, the dawn times would be the winner, no question about it.

However, that's not the way life is, for there will be dark times as well as dawn times, and each has a purpose and a time, and God is in both the dark times as well as the dawn times. He does not merely stay with you when all is well, like some people do. No, He stays with you through the dark moments as well as the dawn ones. He will not leave or forsake you, no matter how dark or hard situations become. God has a solution to every dark situation in your life. The thing about our dark times is that we can become so consumed, frustrated, angry, and overwhelmed by the darkness of the situation until we allow it to overshadow and overpower the truth; which is that God is the light, hope, help, support, and strength to us when dark times come.

Life's dark times are as important as life's dawn times. In some ways, the dark times are of greater value to your walk of faith, for it is in the dark times when faith is tested the most and greatest. It is also in the dark times in life that faith is strengthened, for faith becomes the glue to help you to stand firm, strong, and steadfast in the darkest of times. It is faith which allows you to look beyond the darkness and continue to embrace hope and belief, and it is faith that encourages you to depend on God, His word, promises, and power, regardless of how dark the storm or trouble is. And it is faith which comforts the heart and uplifts the soul in times of darkness. Dark times are not times many would like to engage in. Nevertheless, there is a season and time for the darkness to emerge the same as dawn times. The good news in the dark times is in knowing that God is still God in the dark times as well as the dawn times. Dawn times are the times when all is going well, when life is on the mountaintop instead of the valley. But life does not only consist of mountaintop times; it also has valley times; and it is in the valley where we recognize and appreciate God's goodness, greatness, and grace. He uses the valley, which is often dark times, to serve His purpose and to train us into who He wants and desires us to be.

God is too wise, kind, merciful, caring, and loving to allow anything to come forth that would not be good and best for our lives, even those dark times we face. God is a father, and as a father, He knows what His children lack and need, and He knows that sometimes they need the dark times as well as the dawn times. Consider the following five questions:

- First, consider that if life was always in its dawn times, how would we learn to depend on and trust in the Lord?
- Second, how would we learn about the character of God?
- Third, how would we learn about our own character?
- Fourth, how would our relationship between God and others become stronger, grow, and develop?
- And fifth, how would we learn what it means to be a person only after the heart of God, which are the things of God instead of the things we seek and search out for our own lives?

It's not in the dawn seasons and times in life that any of these five things are learned; only the darkness gives birth to those five things in our lives. The dark times are times which reveal what is often hidden deep in the heart, be it hurt or distrust or other things. Anything which is a hindrance in your life, the dark times cause it to become visible to you whatever it may be.

Do you know it is the cares in your life which often prevent you from moving forward into the life and things God has for you? There are times we all need to remove and clear out the clutter we've been holding on to, things that are unhealthy and unproductive. It is not the dawn that draws us closer to the Lord; it is not in the dawn we learn to trust, depend, and rely on the Lord. It is in the dark times. Do you know that faith is not strengthened in the dawn times, and trust is not developed in the times of ease, comfort, or peace? No, it is in the rough, tough, uncomfortable, and hard times in life; for it is in those times of darkness we cry out and call out to God for help. It's in the dark times we draw nearer and closer to our Heavenly Father. It's in the dark times we seek out His will over our will. It's in the dark times He increases in our life as we decrease. And it's in the dark times, not the dawn, we learn that His grace is sufficient for everything we go through.

Footnote: Even in the dark times, God is there with you and will not leave or forsake you.

Hold On, the Dawn Will Come

Now faith is being sure of what we hope for
and certain of what we do not see.

—Hebrews 11:1

Sometimes, when you have one dark situation after another, waiting on the dawn to come can cause you to feel like it will not happen. If this is how you are feeling today, I encourage you to hold on, don't give up, don't lose heart, don't despair, don't be discouraged, don't be anxious, don't worry, and don't be fearful or fretful; have faith, for the dawn will come. Therefore, hold on and trust in the Lord, and let not your heart be troubled. Before the dawn comes forth, the darkness must have its time as well, for without the darkness there would be no dawn, just as without the night there would be no day. Each has its own time to come and serve its purpose, and it will not be cheated. After the day has run its course, night also must have its time as well, the same as darkness. It's never easy in those dark times before the dawn. However, when the focus is shifted off the darkness of the situation, the power of God's word strengthens you and your faith, which enables you to see the dawn in your situations instead of the darkness. Faith sees what is to be and not what is already. Sometimes, however, when we continue to be in darkness, it is not so easy to hold on in the darkness as we wait for the dawn to spring forth. But there is always the rain before the rainbow, and the cloudiness before the storm. There is also darkness before the daylight.

There are times in life when it looks like the dawn is about to come concerning the troubles and situations in our lives, only to find ourselves still dealing with the darkness of the situation. In fact, there are times when the situation goes from bad to worse, from hard to difficult, from hurtful to painful, from frustrating to stressful, and from dark to darker, with dawn nowhere in sight. Yet that's the way some circumstances, problems, and troubles can become before the dawn. Sometimes things get darker, not better or brighter. However, I have learned in my own darkness before the dawn, the dawn representing my breakthrough from my troubles, that even in the darkest and painful of times, the Lord was with me as my comforter, guide, helper, strength, and supporter. The Lord became my light in the darkness; His quiet and gentle voice calmed my anxious heart and uplifted my troubled soul. The Lord is not only with you in the dawn times of life, He is also with you in the dark times of life. The times when life is rough, tough, and hard to endure; the times when the heart is heavy and troubled, and the mind is uneasy and uncertain, and the soul is restless and unsettled. These are the dark times of life; the times when faith and hope are tested and tried, the times when every bone in your body would like to give up. These are the dark times before the dawn; the times when hope has to encourage itself. These are the dark times in life; the times when prayers go up to the Father, only to remain unanswered and unfulfilled. These are the dark times; the times when you feel alone and uncared for, the times when God is silent, the time when the soul cries out in pain. Yes, these are indeed the dark times; the times when the darkness feels like it is about to choke the life out of you.

Yes, these are the times of darkness; the times when the darkness feels like it is going to win. Yet even in your darkest trouble, consider that God is the light in the darkness, and no matter how dark the situation becomes before it gets better and brighter, you have victory over the darkness, for the Lord is with you, and in Him there is no darkness, only light and hope. It is the hope in Him, His power, and His love that overshadows the darkness. When it comes to your darkest trouble in life, do you know that God is able to turn even the darkest of the darkest trouble into the greatest and brightest blessing?

After all, God is a good and great God who is able to do good and great things in your life. There is nothing too dark He cannot change into an amazing, wonderful, bright, and beautiful blessing. God does not want you to dwell on your troubles, no matter how dark they may be. Instead He wants you, by faith, to see Him in the darkness as a light and hope while you wait on Him and trust Him to bring forth your dawn to your troubles. Today you may be dealing with a dark situation, and if so, I want to encourage you to stay focused on God and His word, not the trouble, and to trust in Him and hold on, for the dawn will come. Remember, sometimes things become darker before the dawn; nevertheless, the dawn will come. The question to you is, do you believe?

Footnote: Remember that out of the darkness the dawn will bloom, for God is with you in both.

God Will Take Care of You

I am the Lord, your God, who takes hold of your right
hand and says to you, Do not fear; I will help you.

—Isaiah 41:13

God is a God of comfort, hope, help, strength, peace, and healing; and these things are but a shadow of what He is. He is
also a God of love and grace, a God who is with you through every
situation, a God who gives you rest and refuge in times of weariness
and trouble. He is a God whose plan is perfect, a God who provides
what you need when you need it. He is a God who never changes,
even when situations and things around you do. He continues to be
the same in spite of your situation. Consider, therefore, that He is the
same God in the good times as well as the dark times. He is a God
that will take care of you; a God of strength, providence, power, and
healing. Nothing you encounter in your life is too hard or impossible for God to do. The question is, do you believe He is? Do you
believe God is able to meet your need in your life no matter what it
looks like or feels like? God is powerful enough to turn the situation
around, even if the situation is dealing with health. God is many
things, and one thing He is, is a healer.

Healing is in the power of the Almighty. Whatever the problem
you face, remember what God is able to do, even if you do not yet
see the results. You are called to walk by faith and not by sight. God
is a healer, and God is always close to you, but He is even closer
to you in times of illness and the uncertainty and discomfort of it.
God is a father, and as a father, He does not want or enjoy the pain

and suffering of His child because of an illness. But even in times of health issues, God is still God, and He still loves and cares about His child, even though His child is going through an illness. In times of health issues, one may not understand the reason behind the illness. The comfort and strength to the soul in such times is in knowing that God is with you to help provide you with what you need to endure. Although we would prefer not to experience any kind of illness, the truth of the matter is that there will be times of illness, and in those times God and His Holy Spirit stay even closer. Not only is God and His spirit closer, they also provide you each day with what is necessary to enable you to get through that day, be it strength in moments of weakness, calmness in times of anxiety, peace in times of struggle, rest in times of weariness, and refuge in times of trouble. Whatever you need and whenever you need it, God is able to supply, for He will never forsake the righteous. Even in illness and sickness, God is at work, and He always has a purpose and plan, even in times of illness. Although you don't always understand the whys for the situation, you can have confidence in God to help see you through.

We say that we want to be more like Jesus, and suffering was a big part of Jesus's life, but even in His suffering, Jesus glorified His Heavenly Father, and so does the suffering of His children. God is too wise and knowledgeable to allow anything to happen without a reason. Nothing comes forth in the lives of His children simply by chance; no, everything is appointed, approved, and arranged by Him before it touches the lives of His children. There's a season and a time for everything to come and to end. God is the time keeper for the start and finish of all, even sickness. When it comes to sickness, God can use what His children go through to help someone who's going through the same thing. Each of us are servants of the Lord, and each of us serve Him in different ways, means, and methods, and only He knows which way and how He will choose to activate the service through you. Sometimes it may be through way of your health or other troubles and situations. God has a reason and purpose for all you go through. One reason may be because He is testing your faith or teaching you to trust, depend, and rely on Him, and His power. Another reason could be because He wants to strengthen your relationship with Him. Only God knows the reason, and so we trust in Him.

God is with you in all things at all times, and He becomes to you what is helpful to you. To the hurting, broken, wounded, and sick, He is a healer, comforter, and shepherd who restores peace to the soul. God is with you in every situation; His presence will give you comfort. His love surrounds you every moment of the day; His strength strengthens you in times of weakness; His peace will guard your mind and heart in times of difficulty; and His word will be a shield and support in times of stress, fear, and uncertainty. God is the source for all you need. He is the God who takes hold of your right hand and says to you, "Be still and know that I am God and I am a healer."

Footnote: You can always trust God to meet your needs.

He's in the Season

To everything there is a season.

—Ecclesiastes 3:1

When times are good be happy,
but when times are bad, consider God has
made the one as well as the other.

—Ecclesiastes 7:14

When it comes to life's seasons, let us consider that every season we have comes at a certain time, and every activity in that season happens at the time it should. Also let us consider that God has made them all, the good ones as well as the not so good. He has a plan and purpose for every one of our life's seasons. From the best to the worst, the Master has a plan and purpose, and He had it before it ever came visible into your life. Consider that every season which enters into your life has been set to arrive at a certain month, day, and time. Every season is set to be by the powerful and mighty hands of the Creator of all time. From the start to the finish, God is in control and in charge, and no one can stop what God begins— no one. Consider that every season you go through is already a season appointed, approved, ordained, and okayed by God. Before it became visible to you, it was already visible to Him.

Though every season is different, consider that each is designed for a particular plan and purpose, even your darkest and difficult ones. With God, even life's darkest and difficult seasons can turn into your brightest and best. Consider that with Him your hardest can become your easiest, while your worst can change into your best. For with God, all things are possible for Him to do. Consider that what is impossible to man is never impossible to Him. God is great and He is powerful; nothing is too hard for Him to accomplish. Consider that every season you experienced, enjoyable or unenjoyable, likable or unlikable, God still had a plan and purpose. Consider that no season, not one, ever arises without God's knowledge. Every season passes by way of His watch before it is released into our lives.

God is too kind, compassionate, caring, and loving to do anything hurtful or harmful. Consider carefully that truth in every season we face and deal with. We will never ever face them alone because He is with us, ready to support, help, and provide whatever is necessary to encourage us to endure until the season is over; and in due time it shall be. The comfort to us in our seasons of life is in knowing we are not alone, for our Heavenly Father is in between us and our seasons, however they may perhaps be. The Lord is not just with us in certain seasons; no, He is with us in all seasons. The Lord does not change; He remains faithful to us, His word, and His promises. When it comes to life's seasons, consider that He is in every season we go through. Everything we go through has been designed to be a part of His greater plan and purpose. God allows nothing to come alive without a reason. Good, bad, hard, or easy, all have His purpose and His plan attached with them.

Every season—be it a season of suffering, grief, sorrow, or joy—is still part of His purpose and plan. Even though we may not understand it all, we can still trust in the truth that the Lord is with us and that in the end He will work it for our good and His glory. There will be times in life when we won't understand the reason for the season, but by faith we're able to look beyond what life's seasons bring because we know who is with us. And who is with us is our Father who is the source of everything we need to carry us through every season. Whatever your season is today, consider that God has a purpose and plan. Consider that He is in the season with you. Consider that you can trust and depend on Him. And last, consider that whatever your season is, God has made them all, and each has a purpose and plan for your life.

Footnote: Even in your darkest season, have faith and confidence that God is with you.

Cheer Up, Don't Lose Heart

A cheerful heart is great medicine.

—Proverbs 17:22

Do not let your heart be troubled.

—John 14:1

E ven in the worst of times, there is a reason to be cheerful in the
midst of it all, because God is still God, and He is still able to
turn the tide in your life, no matter how rough or powerful the tide
is. God can speak a situation into a change. Without any notice, a
situation can suddenly change around for your good and His glory.
Therefore, cheer up, the tide will change, and all will be calm and
quiet down. Don't lose hope, for God has not forgotten or forsaken
you. It is merely not yet the season or time for Him to meet your
need, whatever your need may be. Just because the situation is still
the same as before does not mean that a change in your favor is not
about to take place concerning the matter. Therefore, cheer up and
don't give up, for the tide in your life may be at an all-time high, but
God is still God, and He is able to do anything; for with God, nothing is ever impossible to do. Therefore, cheer up and do not be upset,
frustrated, fearful or fretful; instead be prayerful and praiseworthy
because God is still in control of the matter and He still cares about
you, your life, and your circumstances. Therefore, cheer up and let
not thine heart be troubled, worried, or anxious, for God is still powerful and knowledgeable enough to turn things around.

Because the tide looks the same does not mean it is, because what is, is not what is yet to be. Therefore, cheer up and hold on, for God is still God, and He knows and understands the reason the tide has not yet turned around. Therefore, cheer up and don't lean to your own understanding, but instead trust Him to handle the matter in the way and time He knows to be best for you. Sometimes we think we know what is best, only to discover it really was not. Therefore, cheer up and wait on the Lord; He will give you each day what you need to help you endure as you wait for the tide to change. Remember these things as you wait. First, remember that God is with you every step of the way. Second, remember God is able to meet the need. Third, remember that God loves you and that you are precious to Him. Fourth, remember that God knows what to do. Fifth, remember that God's grace is always sufficient for you no matter the trouble. Sixth, remember there is a season, a time, and a purpose for all things to begin and end. And seventh, remember God's promise is to work all things out and to be with you.

God is a promise keeper, not a promise breaker. He can be trusted to be faithful to every promise He makes. Therefore, cheer up; things will get better because the Master is still in charge of the tide in your life. Today, if you are down because the situation has not changed, I would like to say to you cheer up and don't be discouraged. God is still God, and today may be the day the tide turns in your life; I pray it will. May God bless and strengthen you, and may His peace abide in you.

Footnote: A cheerful heart is a heart that has peace because it rests in the Lord.

He Changes the Impossible to Possible

Everything is possible for him who believes.

—Mark 9:23

All things are possible with God.

—Mark 10:27

E ven when things look to be hopeless and impossible to change, consider that with God all things are possible, even those things that look to be impossible to us. God is a God who is able and wise enough to know how to change every impossible we face in life to a possible. We cannot change those things in our lives which look and feel impossible to change, but the encouragement to us in such times is in knowing that God can. By ourselves we can't, but with God's help, everything is possible, possible that is for him who believes. Mark 9:23 scripture reminds us to consider in our impossible things in life that they can become possible with God's help if we believe in our hearts that He is able to change the impossible to possible.

It seems like our impossible changing into possible depends on what we believe. Therefore, when we find ourselves dealing with those things that look to be impossible, the question to us is, do we believe God is able to change the impossible to possible? It's easy to believe when there is no situation happening, but what about when a situation comes forth that looks and feels like it's a situation or problem impossible to turn around?

There are some troubles which look impossible to work out, even though God's word reminds us in scripture that all things are possible with God. Nothing is too hard for Him to do, nothing. However, there are times when it feels like the impossible is in control and the possible has no chance to be victorious over it. Speaking for myself, I can tell you that I've had moments, seasons, and times when situations looked hopeless and impossible to change in my life. I must admit that those were times when my stress level and anxiety reached an all-time high, until I allowed the word of God to remind me who God was and who I am to Him. God is my Creator and Father, and I am His child, the apple of His eye, whom He loves. Sometimes, in what looks to be an impossible situation, it's easy to forget about the goodness, greatness, and grace of our Heavenly Father. We all need a reminder from time to time to help us to endure the impossible until God changes them into the possible in His time and His way.

Here are some helpful suggestions to help when facing the impossible. First suggestion is to have faith that all things are possible with God, even when they look not so, for faith is not based on what is seen but what is not seen. Hebrews 11:1 scripture states that faith is the evidence of things not yet seen. Second suggestion is to believe, believe all things are possible for Him to do no matter how impossible they seem to be. Mark 9:23 scripture states that everything is possible for Him. Third suggestion is to think positive, for it is right thinking which produces positive actions and attitude. Fourth suggestion is to trust. Trust in God's help, for He is trustworthy; He will never leave or forsake the righteous. Proverbs 3:5 scripture reads, "Trust in the Lord with all your heart and lean not to your own understanding." Fifth suggestion is to pray continually, even if your situation looks impossible, for remember you stand with faith, not with sight. In 1 Thessalonians 5:17 the scripture reads, "Pray continually." The sixth suggestion is give thanks; give thanks even when your situation in life feels impossible to change. Still give thanks to the Lord who is able to change your impossible into possible. For 1 Thessalonians 5:18 reads, "Give thanks in all circumstances, for this is God's will for you in Christ Jesus." Today, if things look impossible, remember that all things are possible with God.

Footnote: God has the power to change the impossible to the possible.

Wow! What about Those Potholes?

God is our refuge and strength, an ever
present help in trouble.

—Psalm 46:1

Recently, while traveling with my husband, we found ourselves playing dodgeball with some large and irritating potholes on our journey. Adding to an already uncomfortable, unpleasant, and uneasy situation was the fact that the traffic was heavy, and the roads were also rough and bumpy. All of these things made the journey stressful, hard, complicated, and overwhelming. What had started off as a pleasant ride suddenly became an unpleasant one.

Without any warning, we found ourselves faced with the unexpected. As my husband managed to maneuver through the unsettling and nerve-racking ordeal, I began to think about how unexpected things, much like the potholes, suddenly come into your life. One moment all is well and then wham! There is a pothole in your pathway. And although potholes have a way of shaking you up, they also have a way of toughening and strengthening you up. Life's potholes and bumps also make you determined to persevere in spite of the hardships of the situation you face.

Life has times of the expected as well as the unexpected. I believe it is the unexpected which teaches, trains, and prepares you to learn how to depend and rely on God's help and power, no matter how many potholes you face on the journey. God will be with you; He will help to direct and navigate you through. You may feel the bumps and roughness, but God will bring you safely through. He will be an ever-present help in the time of life's potholes. And He will use the potholes experience to teach you how to trust in Him, His word, and His power. Life has its share of bumps, potholes, and rough roads for sure. And although it would be great if it was not so, the truth of the matter is that there will be some bumps and potholes on your life's journey. Sometimes it's one bump and pothole after the next, making the journey uncomfortable, difficult, and hard, to say the least. But do you know it's the bumps, potholes, and rough roads you encounter on life's journey which enable you to pray more and to seek out God's help and wisdom?

It is life's potholes, bumps, and rough roads the journey brings your way to test your faith. It's the potholes that lead you to trust and depend on Him. It's the potholes which remind you that God is your refuge and strength. It's those bumps, rough roads, and potholes you engage in on the journey that draw you nearer to God. It's during life's potholes and rough roads which the words, "Never will I leave you or forsake you," are what comforts your soul in the midst of your pothole experience. It's the rough roads you enter into on the journey that help you understand what it means to walk by faith and not by sight. For it is the faith walk which causes you to look past and beyond all the potholes and bumps and see smoother, brighter, and better roads are ahead on the journey. And although there may be some potholes to deal with, the encouragement to your heart is in knowing that you are not alone. For in every bump you face in life, God is with you. He is right there offering His help, support, strength, guidance, and His love. Throughout every bump, pothole, and rough road on your journey, the Lord carries you over and through. None of your life's potholes keep Him standing on the sideline; He is with you holding you up and steady.

Regardless of how hard or tough life's bumps become, remember nothing you face in life is greater or more powerful than God. Life's journey is an adventure, and sometimes the adventure takes us on the road full of potholes. The journey is not always the same, but God is, whether the journey is a time of potholes or a time of ease. God will be with you wherever the journey carries you. Today, whatever potholes you may be facing, remember you are not alone, for God is an ever-present help.

Footnote: When it comes to life's potholes, the good news is that God is with you to get you through life's pothole moments.

He Answered My Call

When I am in distress I call to the Lord.

—Psalm 86:7

I sought the Lord and He answered, He
delivered me from all my fears.

—Psalm 39:4

Life's journey is not always a time of sunshine or smiles. Sometimes it is a time of sadness and weeping. Life's journey will have its ups and downs, but our Heavenly Father is more powerful than anything you face in life. If you trust and allow the Lord to work in your life, you may be shocked and surprised at what He can do for you. Here is some of what He did for my life. When I found myself in distress over the difficult storms I faced in my life, I called on Him, and He invited me to come and take shelter underneath His mighty and powerful wings until the storms passed. He shielded and supported me. He spoke the words, "Be still and know that I am God," into my soul in the time of my storms. With a gentle, soft, and yet firm voice, He gave words of encouragement to my troubled heart.

When I called on Him, He broke the shackles of pain, hurt, and heartache off my life and set me free. He covered me with His love like a blanket. He showed me compassion, concern, and care like I've never known before. He gave me mercy for my misery. He protected and preserved my life from the cruelty, harshness, and evilness of my enemies. He poured His grace down on me like water flowing from a waterfall. He rebuilt my shattered life from the hurt caused by disappointment, discouragement, and dismay. He lifted me up out of the dark pits of life, where the jealousy, envy, and hatred of others had put me. He raised up my weak and fragile body with His powerful right hand. He answered my pleas for help in times of trouble. He restored my soul, refreshed my mind, and renewed my heart. He removed from my life all that were unhealthy, unproductive, and unpleasant. He gave me a reason to rejoice, smile, and laugh.

He showed me what true, real, and unconditional love looked and felt like. He provided me each day with my daily bread. He said that I was beautifully and wonderfully made, in spite of the hurtful and painful words and comments of others. He reminded me that He was with me and would not leave me, that He cared about me and my life. He also reminded me that I was the apple of his eye and that He had a plan and purpose for my life. He gave comfort, confidence, and courage to endure and withstand some of the darkest times in my life. He enabled me to be strong in moments of weakness, loneliness, and uncertainty by reminding me that He is still in control and His grace is still sufficient. He got rid of yesterday's failures, mistakes, and issues by offering new days, dreams, desires, and new ideas. Whatever you need Him to do in your life, today is a good time, chance, and opportunity to call on Him. I called on Him and He answered my call, and He will do the same for you.

Footnote: He is always there for you, ready to answer your call.

He's with You on the Journey

Be strong and courageous. Do not be terrified, do not be
discouraged for the Lord your God will
be with you wherever you go.

—Joshua 1:9

When it comes to your journey in life, you don't know where
the journey will carry you or what is ahead of you on the journey, but you can have confidence in knowing you are not alone on
the journey because the Lord is with you every step of the way. He's
there in the good times as well as the bad. He's there for the best of
times as well as the worst. He's there in the times of laughter as well as
the times of weeping. He's there in the dark times as well as the dawn
times. He's there in the joyful times as well as the sorrowful times.
He's there when the news is good as well as when the news is bad.
He's there when the sun is shining as well as when the rain is pouring. God is with you always regardless; He's not just with you when
things are great and wonderful, but He is also with you when things
are hard, rough, and tough. God is with you through it all, whatever
you encounter on the journey He is there always able and willing to
offer his help, support, and strength when the occasion arises.

We are blessed to have a good, great, generous, and gentle
Shepherd who equips us with what is in our best interest to enable
us to persevere in our darkest and difficult times. The good news
for us on the journey is that we have a Shepherd who goes through
everything we do. He remains faithful; He promised never to leave
or forsake you, and because He is not a liar but is faithful to every

promise He makes. Therefore, you can have confidence that He will do what He promised to do, which is to always be with you when the journey is easy as well as hard. Life is a journey; a journey of faith, belief, hope, trust, and courage. It is also at times a journey of hardships, hurts, pain, grief, trouble, tests, trials, disappointments, and discouragement. It is also a journey of training and learning, and it is also a journey with different seasons which bring different experiences.

However, no matter what comes forth in your life's journey, consider the following. First, consider that God is with you always. Second, consider that God is powerful, trustworthy, and able to take care of you and any situation. Third, consider that God has a plan and purpose for all things, even the painful and hard ones. Fourth, consider that God is in control and charge of you, your journey, and the things you go through on the journey. Fifth, consider that God is able to meet all of your needs. Sixth, consider that God is dependable. And seventh, consider that God loves you.

Life is a journey, and there are many directions the journey can lead you to. Yet whatever direction you find yourself heading to, take comfort in knowing that the Lord is also going as well. Today your journey may have taken you in the direction of sorrow, sickness, and sadness.

Life is a journey of surprises and the unexpected. Life is also a journey with many directions, roads, paths, twists, and turns. Yet no matter the direction you find yourself heading, consider that the Lord is also going as well because He is always with you. Today your journey may have taken you in a direction you would prefer not to have gone, and so my prayer is that your heart not be troubled and your soul strengthened by the assurance that the Lord is with you, and you can trust in His help and provision to see you through.

Footnote: No matter what direction life's journey takes you, be comforted in knowing that God is with you throughout the journey.

Be Still, My Soul, and Know

Be still and know that I am God.

—Psalm 46:10

When one is troubled in heart, when one is worried, when one is anxious, when one is discouraged, when one is fearful, when one is weary, when one is frustrated, when one is stressful, when one is doubtful, when one is unsure and uncertain, when one is hopeless, when one is disappointed, when one is burdened, and when one is weary and weak because of one's situation and circumstance imposed on one from the hardships, heartache, hurt, and difficulties brought on by one's troubles, the words *be still* is not always an easy thing to do. Yet with the word of God and the help of the Holy Spirit, one can be still in the Lord in spite of one's situation. It takes the reminder and remembering of what God is to one's life. For instance, God is good, great, powerful, and present. Yet there are times, in the midst of great suffering and distress, that God's goodness, greatness, power, and presence are not experienced. This is simply because the focus is on the situation, and the troubles and problems of the situation, and what one is feeling, until what and who God is fails to be recognized and acknowledged. God's goodness, greatness, power, and His presence have been shut out and left out because of the things one is going through.

The darkness of the situation, the hardship of the situation, and the pressure from the situation can take a toll on the thoughts, attitude, and actions of the one who is dealing with the situation. When one is under such conditions, it can become increasingly hard to be calm and at peace, let alone to be still. But God knows the soul that is still is the soul where His word and the Holy Spirit can help the mind to stay steadfast on the goodness, greatness, power, presence, and promise of the Lord; and the faithfulness, mercy, compassion, grace, and love of God. It is true that He gives new mercy every day, but it is also true that He has a grace for every situation.

The soul that is stressful, burdened, doubtful, and fearful is the soul unable to comprehend, accept, and feel the goodness, greatness, power, presence, and peace of the Lord. Therefore, in times of trouble, the soul is unable to be still; to be still and know that God is still good, great, powerful, and present. There are some things one must be willing to do. First thing is to submit the situation to the Lord and leave it in His care. Second thing is to focus on the goodness, greatness, and power of the Lord instead of the situation. Focus on God helps the soul not only to be still but also to be at peace. Third thing is to trust; trust in God and lean not to your own understanding about the matter. Fourth thing is to have faith in the goodness, greatness, and love of God. Fifth thing is to believe in the power, knowledge, and wisdom of the Lord to resolve the issue in His way and time. Sixth thing is to have confidence in the word and promises of the Lord. And the seventh thing is to depend on the presence of the Lord and His help.

No matter what life brings, the Lord is with you and ready to help you. Regardless of how dark or painful a situation is, the Lord is still able to help you endure. God understands about you and your life's trouble, and He also knows what to do, when to do it, and how to do it.

He only asks you to be still and know that He is a God that can do everything. With God, all things are possible for Him to do. Nothing has ever been and nothing shall be too hard for God to accomplish. If God could create the heavens and earth and everything above and beyond it; if God spoke and it came to be as He spoke it. If God spread the sky over the earth like a blanket; if God placed the stars in the sky; if God brought forth the sunshine, rain, and snow. If God takes care of the birds in the air and clothes the fields of the earth with grass and wild flowers. If from the flatlands, to the valleys, to the mountains all bear witness to His greatness and power, and if you believe He created all these wonderful and amazing things; and after taking all these things into consideration, don't you think that God is able to take care of any situation in your life? God is able to meet your need; there is nothing the Lord cannot do, even if He has not yet done what you have been praying about. Remember that God's time is not the same as your time, and His wisdom and way are not the same as yours.

Faith is what we are called upon and encouraged to live by and walk by. By faith we look not at what the situation is, but instead we look beyond it and rely and depend upon God to help us in times of life's storms, tests, and troubles. When your spirit can connect with His spirit, you will be able to fully understand what it means to be still in the Lord and know that He is a God in control of every situation in your life. If you can embrace the goodness, greatness, and grace of God, then you will be able to experience the presence and power of the Lord working in you whatever the trouble is. The peace of God will surround you, which helps you to be calm and still instead of stressful and fretful. The soul which trusts in the Lord is the soul that the Spirit enables to be still. So today if your soul is weary and troubled, I say to you to be still and know that God is an ever-present help. That He can do beyond and above all that you can ask of or think, and that He will meet your need. That nothing is hard or impossible for Him to do, and that He is a refuge, rock, and fortress in times of trouble. That He will keep you in perfect peace if your mind stays on Him, and if you put your trust and confidence in Him, His goodness, power, and love. My prayer for you today is that your soul be still in the Lord through His power working in you.

Footnote: Even in times of trouble, your soul can be still in the Lord if you will call on Him to help you.

Trusting God in Trying Times

My flesh and my heart may fail but God is the strength
of my heart and my portion forever.

—Psalm 73:26

Trying times can be times when there seems to be no light at
the end of the tunnel. Everything appears to be in a dark and
motionless state with no relief in sight or at hand. Trying times can
be times of doubt, despair, and discouragement; times of struggles,
stress, and difficulty; times of disbelief and disappointment; and
times of hardships, changes, and challenges. Trying times can be
times of great pressure, fear, and worry; times of pain and suffering.
Yet in the midst of the emotions and feelings of it all, trying times
can also be times of reminding one's self about God's love, goodness, greatness, grace, and faithfulness. Trying times can be times of
remembering His power, promises, and provisions. Trying times can
be times of growth in one's faith and relationship with God and others. Trying times can be times of teaching and learning how to trust.
Trying times can be times of self-examination through the word of
God; times of meditation, times of commitment, and times of surrendering to the Holy Spirit. Trying times are not easy times, but
they can be endurable times with God, the word of God, and the
Holy Spirit's help.

Life will have trying times, but it will also have God. Problems,
troubles, tests, and trials will come, but they come not to break or
hurt one but to teach one about the character of God and His love.
It is unrealistic to think or believe there won't be any situations or

circumstances that will be trying times because one believes. In fact, it is the trying times which help to develop, shape, and mold one's faith and character. It is also trying times which show things about you which hinder you from being fruitful in the Lord. Trying times draw the soul nearer and closer to the Lord. You know the more one learns about God, the more one wants to learn; and the more one focuses on God, the less one focuses on one's situation.

God can accomplish His will in the trying times, as well as the times of ease, for God is always in both working for one's good and His glory. Trying times are the times that teach one to trust in God to meet the need. Trying times are also humbling times for the prideful soul. They're also times which remind one that God is the source and reason for everything one has, not one's position, title, or degree, but it is all because of God. This truth is something which will serve one to always remember before one comes down with the disease known as "Look at what me, myself, and I did." God wants to be trusted in the trying times of life.

Here are twelve things to remember about him in trying times that will help:

- First, remember that God loves you.
- Second, remember that God is an ever present help.
- Third, remember God is powerful.
- Fourth, remember God is able to meet the need.
- Fifth, remember God is good and wise.
- Sixth, remember God's Holy Spirit is in you, ready to lead, guide, direct, comfort, support, and strengthen you.
- Seventh, remember God is merciful and compassionate.
- Eighth, remember God is faithful to his word and promises.
- Ninth, remember God is with you, you're never alone to face anything by yourself.
- Tenth, remember that God's grace is sufficient, even in trying times.
- Eleventh, remember God is the God of possible not impossible, for nothing is too hard for him to do, nothing.
- Twelfth, remember that God is trustworthy.

Trying times come to all of us at some time or another. But we can take comfort in knowing that the Lord is with us. When things become hard and tough, we can come to him for rest, refuge, and refreshment. Today, if you are dealing with trying times, remember there is one who understands and who is able to help if you would trust in Him. That one is Jesus Christ, who also had trying times in His life while on this earth. May the peace of God dwell in you as you trust in Him.

Footnote: God does not leave us in trying times. He is there for us, no matter what.

The Walk through Life

I will fear no evil, for you are with me.

—Psalm 23:4

The walk through life is a walk that takes one through many things. Sometimes it is a walk that is not always enjoyable or easy. It is a walk that at times can drain, weaken, and sap the energy from the soul; a walk that can be exhausting and emotional. It is a walk that at times can be unbearable and uncomfortable; a walk which can weigh heavy on the heart. It is a walk of despair, desperation, and disgust. At times it can be an overwhelming, unpleasant, and unhappy walk. Sometimes the walk can be a walk of dismay, disbelief, and discouragement. At times the walk can change to a walk of sadness, sorrow, suffering, and grief. Other times the walk can be a walk which sends shivers down the spine. The walk of life at times can be a walk of coldness, bitterness, and frustration. At times it can become a walk of struggles and difficulties; a walk of tears, weeping, and pain. The walk can challenge the faith at times, and the walk through life can be a walk mixed with a combination of emotions and feelings from all that the soul encounters and faces.

Even though the walk can carry one through the valley of darkness, despair, disappointment, and death, the comfort to the soul is that it is a walk one walks not alone, for it is a walk that the Lord walks with one. The good and great Shepherd walks with one. Wherever the walk leads, and whatever the walk brings forth into one's life, one needs never to be fearful or afraid, for the Lord—who is loving, caring, and compassionate—walks through everything one walks through as well. The Lord is on the walk through life with one. He is always on the walk ready to help, protect, and provide whatever the soul on the walk will need to be able to persevere. Though the walk of life is many things, it is also a walk that the Lord walks with you. Therefore, you need not be fearful or afraid, for the Lord is always on your walk through life. He's there ready to protect, provide, and comfort you on your walk through life.

Footnote: The walk of life is a walk one can be certain and sure that one is never alone, for the Lord is always with one.

Be Still, God's Working It Out

Be still and know that I am God.

—Psalm 46:10

Sometimes you can become so overwhelmed with life and its various situations that you are unable to be still and know that God is still in control. Life can throw you some curveballs from time to time that can cause you to feel like you are caught up in a powerful whirlwind with no way to escape. The things you don't understand or know the reason for are what you usually question and wonder about. Not only do you lack understanding for the situation you are in, you worry, stress, panic, fret, and often become anxious and frustrated about it. There is no peace, calmness, or quietness to be had in your heart when you are dealing with all of the above, like worry and stress, which not only steal your peace but your joy and your rest. Scripture constantly urges you not to worry, not to be anxious, and to not let your heart be troubled, if the mind, heart, and soul are to stay in a peaceful and calm state in times of various life situations. Some situations you face in life are because of something you did or because of others; some are a time of testing and training from the Lord, and others are from the evil one. Yet God is still able to work all things out, if you will stand firm and steady in your faith. Therefore, do not be doubtful or troubled in heart; but instead believe in the goodness, greatness, generosity, and grace of God who is able to do more than you can ever think, imagine, or hope for. Even when emotions cause you to feel like this is impossible, the Holy Spirit reminds you that nothing is impossible for the God who is Creator of the universe. Surely if you believe in God and all of what He has done, then certainly you can believe that He has the power, wisdom, knowledge, and ability to work out your troubles and problems. But you must trust him to work the situation out, even when things go from bad to worse, from hard to difficult, from hurtful to painful, and from dark to darker. Trust Him in spite of it all, for God is in control, and He's on your side regardless of what is now.

There is a solution just waiting to come forth in His season and time. In the meantime, why not be still and know that He's working it out in the way He knows is best for you. Just because you have not gotten the answer to your prayer, it doesn't mean He's not working out the matter according to His plan, purpose, and will. God works all things together for your good and his glory. He may not work it out the way you want or desire, but you can be certain that He will work it out in His time, way, and season. To every situation is a solution, and to every season is a set time for the beginning and the end to every situation, trouble, trial, problem, and storm in life. It's not always easy or comfortable on life's journey because we have no idea what may come forth for us to face or cope with. But one great truth we hold on to is in knowing that God knows, and He already has a plan with a solution and season for the situation to be resolved at His time. Nothing happens on life's journey without God's approval and permission. There are never any surprises or the unexpected for God; and He's never caught off guard, shocked, or unprepared to deal with whatever comes forth in our lives because He knows everything even before it happens. God is in control and in charge, not us or our situations, no matter how they appear to be. God is still in the midst doing what He knows is best for us, even if we don't see or understand. We will never fully understand what He does in certain situations, but we can trust Him to work it out for our good because He is our Heavenly Father, and He cares for us and loves us deeply and compassionately. Though the situation you may be in today is not what you expected, and some days are harder than others, consider that the Lord is with you through it all.

He will continue to be with you, for He is there in every situation and season of your life. He's not only with you, He's also providing what is necessary to enable you to endure every day. He is the giver and source of everything you need in your life and on your life's journey. God knew and knows every single thing that is and will be part of you and your life's journey. He will never leave or forsake you, no matter how rough, tough, or rocky life becomes. God is there; He promised to be with you, and He never breaks a promise but is faithful to fulfill it in His time and His way. Grumbling, complaining, crying, weeping, overeating, stressing, or being miserable won't hurry or convince God to operate on your set time. So why not consider to do as the word suggests, which is do not worry, fret, fear, or be anxious and do not let your heart be troubled or discouraged. Instead trust in God who is in control, and be still and know that God loves you and He understands what to do and when.

Footnote: Sometimes it is good to put life and life's situations not only into perspective but also into the hands of the one who knew how to create the whole universe and everything in it. For if He had the greatness, power, and knowledge to do that, then why not trust Him to take care of you and your situation, whatever it may possibly be.

Not Alone on the Journey

God is our refuge and strength, an ever
present help in times of trouble.

—Psalm 46:1

Never will I leave you, never will I forsake you.

—Hebrews 13:5

God wants you to have a joyful, peaceful, content, and confident life with the assurance that you are never alone on your life's journey. God's word and promises give you absolute assurance that He is an ever-present companion and helper on your side, no matter what the journey brings forth or where the journey leads. There are times, however, when you may feel alone, forgotten, and forsaken. There also may be those times when you not only feel alone but may also think, wonder, and question if God cares or is even concerned about you and what you are going through. Unanswered prayers and waiting on His help can at times begin to take a toll on the mind, heart, and soul. When emotions and feelings begin to run high, and when self begins to listen to self and follows self instead of the word of God and the Holy Spirit, and when it appears that everything is coming at you from all directions, and when it feels like your back is up against the wall, and when it seems like God is silent, it's easy to feel helpless, hopeless, and alone, especially when the heart is troubled over what is happening. But we are never alone, even if we feel like we are. God's promise is to be with you, even to the end of time.

God is not a man that He should lie or break a promise. What God promises is done. He has the power, wisdom, knowledge, and ability to do anything. Nothing is too hard or impossible for God, who is Creator of both the heavens and earth, and all that is in it and beneath it. If in times of situations we could hold in our hearts and let it take root that God is powerful and able to do more than you could think of or even imagine, then your emotions would not make you feel like you're alone in times of hard and difficult situations and troubles. God is faithful, true, and trustworthy in both His word and promises. Whatever He said and promised to do, God shall do. And what He promised was to be there for you in the unpleasant times as well as the pleasant times.

Through all we face in life, be it joyful or sorrowful, He's there by your side because He loves and cares about you. Everything about you and your life matters to God, and you can always rely on Him. You can also have total confidence and contentment in His love and concern about you and your life's situations. No matter how dark or difficult they may be, in his time and way, the darkness will turn to dawn and the difficulty will change to delight. For to everything is a season and time to begin and to end. God knows the time to begin and to end, for He has appointed and approved both the beginning and ending. No season in your life will start before its time, and none will stop before it should, because the Master is over both the set time to come forth and the set time to be finished. Everything is in the Master's hand and under His control, not yours or mine. Sometimes things may look bleak, but God is still there, and He knows what to do, but we must believe and trust Him to meet the need, even if things look bleak at the moment. There is hope in every situation you go through because that hope rests in the Lord. God is good, and His goodness never changes toward you, even when life is challenging. God meets you right in the midst of the challenges. He never leaves you to face or deal with anything that arises in your life. He is there and will be to the end. Life may be unpredictable and uncertain at times for sure. However, God can be counted on to be there for you. God is not ruthless; He understands how some troubles can be stressful and overwhelming at times. Therefore, He invites you to come and dwell in Him; and He will give you release, rest, refuge, and refreshment for your soul, if you take Him up on His invitation to come and be restored and renewed in body, mind, heart, and soul.

We all have or have had moments and times in our lives when we wanted to escape to some place where we could immediately feel relaxed, rested, revived, regenerated, safe, and secure from the struggles and difficulties that life sometimes brings. How great it would be not to deal with some of the stuff that enters into our lives, but the truth about life is that as long as you live, there is always going to be something you would prefer not to be in your life. Jesus told his disciples that in this world there would be times of trouble. So there is no way to escape the big T, for sooner or later it will come. Trouble does not discriminate. Trouble comes and goes wherever, whenever, and to whomever it chooses. But God has promised to be with you in troubled times, and He does not change like the shifting of the wind. If He promised to do something, you can have complete faith in him to do so. Not too many people do what they promise to do because some promises are only made to get something out of what was promised. However, God is not people; He is God who not only promises but keeps and fulfills all He ever promises. God never promised us that life would be easy or that every day would be a day of sunshine, or a time of nothing but laughter, or that there would never be any valleys or deserts to journey through or rough roads to travel. But what He did promise was to see you through everything life's journey carried you through, and that's a promise your heart can take comfort in, whatever life brings to you. You will be able to persevere and endure because God is with you, and His grace is sufficient for every situation that you face.

Footnote: Life and life's situations are not always a time of ease, but the comfort to us in life and its situations is in knowing that we can trust God to be there with us.

Consider He's in It All

When times are good be happy but when times are bad,
consider God has made the one as well as the other.

—Ecclesiastes 7:14

When there's sunshine instead of clouds, there's singing, praising, and rejoicing; but when there are clouds, the singing, praising, and rejoicing seem to vanish and are replaced by weeping, complaining, worrying, and fearing. When the good, great, enjoyable, and comfortable times are no longer so, often God is not viewed in the same way as when times are good. However, God is the same when times are good and bad, and consider that He has made them both. Both the good and the bad are designed for a purpose and a plan for the life, character, growth, and development of his children.

Life's good times are wonderful for sure, but it's not in the good times relationships are deepened between the Father and His children. It's not in the good times that trusting Him is learned. It's not in the good times that knees so often bend and heads look upward. It's not in the good times that faith is strengthened. It's not in the good times that God's promises are depended and relied on the most. It's not in the good times that His word is held the closest in the mind and heart. It's not in the good times that the words, "Be still and know that I am God," touch the depths of the soul in a powerful and profound way. It's not in the good times that who God is and what God is has the greatest impact upon the soul. And it's not in the good times that the sufficiency of God's grace is truly experienced and understood.

No, it's in the bad times when things are dark, dull, dreary, cloudy, and gray that trust is developed, relationships are made stronger, character is built, belief is proven and productive, and faith is tried and tested. It's in the bad times that God is acknowledged and recognized as the source for everything needed in life. It's in the bad times that the goodness of God shines the greatest. And it's in the bad times that His love is shown to be unconditional; His care, compassion, and mercy have no end, and His faithfulness to His word and promises is great and trustworthy. It is life's dark times that make His children become humble in spirit and soul and to be great servants for the Lord to others.

Good times are a blessing, but bad times are an even greater blessing because they draw His children nearer and closer to Him. They also draw out what is bad, unhealthy, and unproductive in and to the life of His children. Bad times are times of troubles, trials, tests, problems, and situations; times which often are hard, painful, difficult, stressful, and overwhelming. Yet these are the times which train up some of the greatest soldiers for the army of the Lord and the work of the Lord. God's love is too deep for His children and His wisdom too great not to know what they need to become like Jesus. Life's journey is not one of only good times but also bad times; and each works together according to God's will, purpose, and plan. Consider therefore that when times are good and when times are bad that God is in the midst of both.

Footnote: God will be with you in both the good times and bad times.

There Is Refuge for the Soul

The Lord is good, a refuge in times of trouble.

—Nahum 1:7

Blessed are all who take refuge in him.

—Psalm 2:12

We all, from time to time, need a refuge for our souls; a refuge to console and calm the soul when life's journey is confronted with the powerful and strong winds of life's storms and situations. It is the challenges and demands in such times which often prompt the soul to seek support and refuge. The good news for the soul who wants refuge is that there is a refuge to come and dwell; a refuge for the soul in times of life's troubles. There is refuge for the soul to relax, unwind, and enjoy the goodness of the Lord. There is refuge for the soul that is in bondage and shackles over the cares of life. There is refuge for the soul who desires comfort. There is refuge for the soul to be able to reflect, regroup, and rethink. There is refuge for the oppressed and confused. There is refuge for the soul to have perfect peace. There is refuge for the soul in need of rest. There is refuge for the soul to be renewed and regenerated. There is refuge for the hurting, broken, and wounded soul. There is refuge for the weary and troubled. There is refuge for the weak to be strengthened; a refuge for the mind to be refreshed and rejuvenated. There is refuge for the soul that is lost and uncertain. There is refuge for the distressed, discouraged, and disappointed soul. There is refuge for the soul that is heavily burdened and overwhelmed. There is refuge for the soul who wants to escape the day-to-day pressures of life. There is refuge for the soul who craves for a time of quietness, tranquility, and serenity. There is refuge for the soul whose heart is troubled. There is refuge for the fallen, unsure, and confused. There is refuge for the soul who wants to be rescued and delivered. There is refuge from the difficulties and hardships of life's situations. There is refuge for the suffering, sorrowful, and sick. There is refuge for the soul who wants shelter and support in times of life's storms. There is refuge for the soul of the believer, no matter the situation, and that refuge is God. He is a refuge for the souls of all who believe and trust in Him.

Footnote: Psalm 62:8 reads, "God is our refuge."

God Is There in All Situations

The Lord was with Joseph and he prospered, and
he lived in the house of his Egyptian Master.

—Genesis 39:2–3

There are problems and troubles in life that at times are painful and hard to deal with. Problems, and at times the pain and heartaches from those problems, can come from others. This is a deeper pain, a pain that cuts deep into the heart, a pain that grieves the soul, a pain that weighs heavy on the mind. These are the pains caused by those who oftentimes are close to one, like one's friends and family. Joseph is a man whose pain came from the hands of his family. Joseph's brothers didn't like him, and they wanted to kill him. This thought stayed on his brothers' minds and hearts, and so they planned and waited for such a chance and opportunity to carry out their thoughts. However, unknown to them, God also had a plan for Joseph. Out of their plan to do evil, God had a plan through their plan to bring about good. Do you know that God can work those whose hearts are evil to bring forth good for the one who the evil plans are meant for? After all, God knows everything about the minds and hearts of everyone, even what is behind every smile.

Joseph's brothers perhaps were full of smiles and laughter right before they threw him into the pit with the intent to harm him, because they hated him. Even in the midst of Joseph's tears and pleading to be taken out of the pit, it had no effect on them. Joseph's pain was a source of his brothers' joy. Not one of his brothers lifted a hand to help him, not one. Joseph was in pain, and it gave his brothers a time of happiness. However, God had a plan and a promise for Joseph's pain. Joseph's pain from the pit his brothers threw him in was only phase one of God's plan and promise. Even in the pit, God was with Joseph and watching over him and protecting him. It was because of God that Joseph's brothers took him out of the pit and sold him to be a slave for money. The story about Joseph is a story where pain and purpose were all part of God's plan. It is a story where Joseph's pain meets God's plan, purpose, provision, and promise. God never left Joseph, even in his hard and painful times. God was with Joseph, and Joseph prospered. This teaches that even in painful and hard times, the Lord is with one, and He can make one prosper even in painful and difficult times.

In Genesis 37:2–3 it describes Joseph as a young boy who did not ask for the trouble he got in his life. However, God was with Joseph, for He had a plan for all of Joseph's pain and hardships. God's plan carried Joseph from the pit he was put in to die because his brothers hated Joseph and were jealous of him. But God's plan met Joseph's pit experience. God's plan took Joseph from the pit to being sold into slavery into the land of Egypt. This also was part of God's plan for Joseph, even though it was a painful and hurtful time for Joseph who had been mistreated by his brothers, then sold as a slave to work in a strange land far away from his father, family, and friends. Yet this was all part of God's plan for Joseph's life. While in Egypt, Joseph experienced some painful situations. He went to prison because of a lie told on him by the wife of the man who Joseph worked for and whose home Joseph lived in. It took the pain of Joseph being thrown in a pit and going to prison before Joseph ended up in the palace as prime minister over Egypt. All of these things Joseph encountered in his life were all part of God's plan.

God's hand was in the midst of all Joseph went through, but Genesis 39:2 points out that God was with Joseph. God is also with us as we go through things in life. Sometimes, as painful and hard as some situations can be, we can have confidence and hope that God is with us and He is still the one in control, not us or the trouble we sometimes face. Whether it is trouble because of us or someone else, at the end of the day, God has a plan for it all, even the pain and misery from the trouble we may face. Consider that there is a plan and purpose for it all. Through the events in Joseph's life and his distress, Joseph was promoted to the position of prime minister in the land of Egypt. God can turn our troubled times into a blessing. God's plan and purpose for Joseph's life took him from the pit to the prison and from the prison to the palace, where he was promoted to the position of prime minister. God was with Joseph; He was present, and He took care of Joseph. God provided for Joseph, and God allowed Joseph to prosper and those around him who he worked for.

Even in painful and hard times God still helps and He also provides. Because of God's plan and Joseph's pain, he was able to save a nation in crisis as well as his family, and his brothers who meant him harm. God's plan was good, not only for Joseph but for others as well. God's promise is to be with us at all times and in all things. This promise is a promise that is trustworthy, unlike the promises of man. God's promise is dependable, and His plan and purpose shall be fulfilled even if that plan includes a time of pain and hurt. Consider that out of Joseph's pain, God gave him the position of prime minister, and out of Joseph's hurt, He gave him happiness; and both were birthed out of Joseph's pain and God's plan.

Footnote: Even in painful times, God is with you, and He has a plan for your life.

He's Our Dwelling in Life's Storms

Lord, you have been our dwelling place,
throughout all generations.

—Psalm 90:1

Whatever storm blows into our lives, we need not fear, fret, or panic because God is on our side; He knows the storm, and He has a solution already. And when the storm becomes overwhelming, He will be our dwelling place. Every moment of our lives is in the hands and the care of God, and that includes our storms of life. There is not a single storm that God is unaware of. He knew it would be a storm and the purpose for it before the storm ever came into existence. God knows all things; therefore, nothing ever escapes Him. God knows what will be before it is. His knowledge is deeper than the deepest ocean. God is awesome; He is a great and amazing God who has the power to do anything. All things are under Him, and He is over everything, even the storms that come into our lives. When it comes to the storms in our lives, let us consider the following two things about God. First, that God is powerful. God can do above and beyond what you could ever think or imagine. Second, consider that all things are possible for God to do, and that means our storms, no matter how strong the storm appears to be. The storms we may face may be great, but God's mercy and grace are greater. Even when our storms may reach their highest peak, there is a God that will see us through, if we will only believe and trust in Him to do so. The battle of life's storms belongs to God, and He is able to win the battle. However, in the midst of our storms, we are blessed to know that God is a dwelling place for the soul to come and dwell in time of the storm; a place where the soul can relax and regroup. It is a place without any interruption; a place for the heavy burdened, the oppressed, hurting, and suffering. God can always be trusted in the storms of life. There is no storm stronger or more powerful than God is. There is not a storm too hard for him to deal with. God can still calm and quiet every storm in your life. God is in control of the storm; the storm is not in control of Him. No matter how overwhelming life's storm becomes, the force of the storm will not overpower the one who believes in and belongs to God. God is on the side of His people, ready to protect, shield, and shelter them in the time of the storm. No matter how rough or tough the storm may become, it will not overcome or defeat the soul that is a child of the Most High.

The storm or storms will never gain victory, for the victory is already the Lord's. That's why God says to be still and know that He is God. He is able to say the words, "Be still, calm down and quiet down," and the storm will obey the words commanded of it. Every storm knows the voice of its Creator and Master. Life's storms bow down to the Almighty, they become humble before Him because He has the authority over them and the power to demand the storm to do what He wants and wills to be so. The storm has neither any power or will, except what is given by God who has a purpose, plan, and reason for every storm life brings forth—be it the storm of trouble, test, trial, illness, sorrow, suffering, or pain. Whatever storm enters into the life of his child, the comfort to the heart and peace to the soul is in knowing that God is with him or her, and He is in charge of the storm, regardless how it seems or feels. The good news is that when life's storms arise, the believer is never alone, for God is also there right by the believer's side, ready and able to help. Whatever help is necessary to enable the believer to weather the storm, God is able to provide. God shall meet the need of His child in the time of his or her storm, and He will not let him or her down. God is reliable and dependable. The believer can always count on Him to be there to help in the time of the storm, regardless of how long it lasts or how hectic it may become before God commands the storm to be still and quiet down. When God speaks these words to the storm, the storm will obey its Master. No storm will continue or last a minute, moment, or second past what it is ordered to do, by the one who has the power to speak, and what is spoken from the mouth of God will become so, for all creation must obey and honor its creator. The rising of the most powerful and mighty storm of the believer, be it a storm of trouble or a storm of suffering, cannot harm or destroy the soul that has faith in God, His word, and His promise. The storm is unable to weaken the soul whose focus is on God and not the rushing waters of the storm in its life.

The more the focus is on God, the less control and power the storm is able to have on the mind, which means the storm will decrease in the mind, while God and who God is will increase. This allows the soul of the believer to have confidence and trust in God. God wants his child to trust him when he or she is in a storm. He wants the believer to call out to Him and to look to Him as the source who is able to sustain and help in such times. God wants the believer to depend on Him for support and deliverance. God has given the Holy Spirit to all who believe in Him, to be there to guide, lead, direct, comfort, council, and to help the believer through the storms of life. He, the Holy Spirit, will order the believer's steps in the storm if the believer will surrender to the Holy Spirit. Life's storms will come, but we don't have to face any storm alone because God our Creator, Father, Protector, Provider, Helper, and Shepherd will carry us through. We need not be anxious, fearful, worried, or doubtful, for God will never leave or forsake His people in the time of their storms. Consider that to every storm there is a season and time to begin and to end. God is in the storm and the season, and He will bring you out like pure gold when the storm has run its course and served its purpose and time, according to the Master's will, purpose, and plan. No storm is ever the same, for each comes with a different assignment and purpose to be fulfilled. Only God, who is all-knowing and wise, knows and understands the reason for all things, even life's storms that come to his people. Some storms are harder on the soul to endure than others, and some last longer. In fact, some go from bad to worse and from dark to darker. But the encouragement to the heart is that in such times, the soul has a dwelling place, a hiding place, a place of serenity, a place of rest, a place of quietness, and a place of protection from the elements of the storm. It is a place to refresh, restore, renew, regenerate, and revive the soul that is weary and weak from the storm in his or her life. This dwelling place is a place to escape the storms of troubles, trials, tests, and problems. It is a place where the peace, presence, and love of God cover the soul like a blanket. It is a place where all who believe can enter into during the time of the storm, and that place is in the Lord, who is our dwelling place.

Footnote: Be comforted in knowing that God is with us through every storm in our lives.

Life Changes, but God Doesn't

Jesus Christ is the same yesterday,
and today and forever more.

—Hebrews 13:8

Never will I leave you; never will I forsake you.

—Hebrews 13:5

Life isn't always a time of pleasure or peace, for it can also be a time of problems and pain. Life isn't always a time of laughter; it can also be a time of loss. Life isn't always a time of happiness; it can also be a time of hardships. Life isn't always a time of dawn; it can also be a time of darkness. Life isn't always a time of goodness; it can also be a time of grief. Life isn't always a time of sunshine; it can also be a time of storms. Life isn't always a time of triumph; it can also be a time of trouble. Life can be a time of various situations and circumstances which can cause great suffering, difficulties, and challenges. But if it was not for life's tough and rough times, we would never learn to trust in, depend on, and rely on God. If life had only times of joy and never times of weeping, sadness, or sorrow, how could we truly understand what it means to have the comfort and compassion of a God who gives His comfort and compassion in all situations and at all times? In times of sorrow and sadness, only God truly knows the depths of the pain, heartache, and hurt inside the heart and soul of the one going through such a time; and only God knows how to comfort and care for that soul. God is the Father of compassion and the God of all comfort, who comforts us in all of our situations and seasons of life. It is in the bitterness of life, not the sweetness of life, where the soul seeks to draw nearer and closer to God. It's in the trenches of life, when the soul is surrounded by troubles, trials, and tests, where trust is learned and faith is tested. It's in the struggles and hard times of life that the soul understands that God's amazing grace is sufficient in all situations and seasons of life.

Life isn't always a time of singing; sometimes it is a time of suffering. But it's in the time of suffering that the soul can be strengthened, comforted, and refreshed by the Lord. In the good times as well as the bad, unkind, unpleasant, and difficult times God is near. He's there in the midst covering His child with His love, like the garment on his or her body. Life isn't always a time of sunshine; it can be a time of storms. Storms, that at times, can feel like the storm is about to swallow the soul. Yet it is out of the storm God speaks to the soul with the assurance that He is in control of the storm, so there's no need to be afraid, for the storm is under the authority, control, and power of him. Life's storm is not something any soul desires, wants, or prefers, for some storms can be hard to endure, as well as painful. But to every storm there's a season, time, and purpose for the storm to come forth with a mission and assignment to fulfill and complete. Character cannot be built, developed, produced, and established in a time of ease and relaxation, but it is through the storm and the experience of the things that come with the storm that develop character. It's in the storm trust is learned, faith is strengthened, courage is risen up, and hope is inspired to hold on. When it comes to life, it's true that it isn't always a time of rejoicing, for it can be a time of tears and crying. But through the rejoicing or the tears, God is present; He is an ever-present help in whatever life's situations may be or become. We have no control over the changes that take place in our lives. However, the good news for the believer is that God does not change; He remains the same loving, faithful, caring, and compassionate God, full of mercy and grace who is able to help.

Footnote: Life is full of changes, but whatever changes we face, as long as we stay connected and in tune with God, His word, and His promises, we will be okay.

Trusting Him to Take Care of You

I will instruct thee and teach thee in the way which thou
shall go. I will guide thee with mine eye.

—Psalm 32:8

God will direct your path if He is trusted to do so. Even though
you may not always notice or pay attention, your Heavenly
Father is watching over you, including your coming and going. He's
also looking out for you in times of trouble and other life situations.
No matter how difficult or challenging they are, God is with you and
watching out for you and over you. I guess you can say that He has
your back at all times, even when you feel alone. Psalm 46:1 reminds
you that God is ever-present, which assures you that He is watching
over you even when situations and circumstances indicate that He's
not. Sometimes your emotions can have you believing, thinking, and
feeling all kind of things. After all, emotions are guided mainly by
what self is experiencing and seeing, based on self-understanding of
the situation, which is very limited, to say the least. Proverbs 3:5–6
states to trust in the Lord with all your heart and lean not to thine
own understanding. But in all your ways acknowledge him, and he
will make your paths straight. God has your back; He's watching
over you and protecting you from harm and danger. He knows what
is before you and what is ahead of you, and that's why He urges you
to trust in him and not self, for self only knows what self wants and
desires. But it is the Lord who truly knows and understands you, your
heart, and your situation that is before you. He and He alone is able
to meet your need, certainly not self because self is unable to help its

own self or to do anything without the wisdom and help of the Lord. One thing self is capable of doing is making a mess, when it will not surrender self to God and the Holy Spirit to guide, lead, direct, and order its steps, for self is a good negotiator when it comes to what self thinks is best for self. Self-thinking, self-ideas, and self-seeking can only go one way, which is to fail. Misery, heartache, and heartbreak await the one who trusts to go his way instead of God's way.

God is an expert on what to do about any situation that comes forth into your life. And guess what? He already knows what to do, and He does not need any advice, assistance, or help from you concerning the matter. Sometimes one can be wise in its own way of thinking about what to do about a certain situation or problem. But consider this: God's thinking is not the same as yours. One more thing to consider is His time is not the same as your time to operate in. When it comes to the completion and end of any situation you face, God will not be rushed to give you a solution, but He will watch over you and provide what you need to enable you to endure the situation you are in until the reason for the situation has served its purpose. Only God, who allowed the situation, knows when it will be over. Everything from God comes not to harm or hurt you, but it comes with a specific plan and purpose that must be fulfilled in his chosen season and time. God is a God of order; therefore, every situation that comes is at the time He set. With God, there's nothing that happens without His knowledge of it. Before you were born, God already had designed a plan and purpose for your life. He sets the time for all things, and when He sets the time for anything, it will run its course according to His will, not yours. God loves you, and His desire is to make you more like Him. He wants a close and deep relationship with you, and He wants you to walk by faith and not by sight. God wants you to believe in Him, His character, and His power. He wants you to trust him for what to do concerning matters in your life. He wants your life to reflect him and not that of the world. When situations come, remember that God always has a reason, purpose, and season for the arrival and a time for the departure as well. The more God is trusted, the less self is, and the better we will feel physically, mentally, spiritually, and emotionally.

Footnote: When you don't know what to do about your situation, why not trust God, who knows what to do about everything, even your situation, if you would only trust Him.

Trusting Him in the Midnight Times

About midnight Paul and Silas were praying and singing hymns to God, and the other prisoners were listening to them.

—Acts 16:25

Midnight times can be difficult, discouraging, depressing, distressful, doubtful, and dark. Midnight times can be challenging, uncomfortable, and uncertain. Midnight times can be times of waiting, weeping, wondering, and worry; times of anger and anxiety; and times of fear and frustration. Midnight times can be can be times of pruning, times of clearing away what is unhealthy and unproductive for one's growth and development in the Lord. Midnight times can be times of soul searching, seeking, surrendering, sustaining, submitting, and strengthening. Midnight times can be times of training, testing, teaching, and trusting. Midnight times can also be times of prayer, praising, singing, and remembering that even in the midnight times, God is with one and He is in control of the midnight times in life, the same as He is in the dawn times. Do you know that midnight times in one's life are just as important, useful, and valuable as the dawn times of life? The Lord can use both of them to serve His purpose for one's life. It's the midnight times which teach the soul what it means to depend on the Lord and rely on his promises. It's also the midnight times that teach one what it means to truly trust in the Lord. It's the midnight times which train one in one's faith walk. It's also the midnight times that teach one the wisdom in seeking the Lord on matters before one seeks out self. It's also the midnight times which show one how to have courage in spite of one's situation. It's in the midnight times where the Lord becomes the center of one's life and situation. It's in the midnight times where self decreases and the spirit of God increases. It's in the midnight times that one keeps on one's knees, calling out in prayer to the Lord. It's in the midnight times one learns the depth of God's love, goodness, and greatness. It's in the midnight times that God's mercy shines brighter than ever; and it's in the midnight times that praise is the sweetest tasting to the mouth, the greatest comfort to the heart, and uplifting to the soul.

It's the midnight times when the spirit longs to embrace the love of God. It's in the midnight times when the soul takes refuge and shelter in the Lord. It's in the midnight times where the weary, stressful, and hurting soul can come and dwell in the shadow of the Almighty, because it is there in one's midnight times that one's soul can be satisfied, calm, and comforted. It's in the midnight times one is able to be shielded from the hardships of the midnight because one is able to take cover underneath the powerful wings of one's Master, Creator, and Heavenly Father, who is able to protect and provide for one until the midnight has passed away and the dawn has come. Midnight times are not great times, but they can be productive times, teaching times, and humble times. They can also be times of learning how to be still and to wait on the Lord's timing. It is the midnight times which help one's focus to stay on the Lord instead of the midnight. It is the midnight that causes one to be humble in the dawn times and not become proud or arrogant, and to give praise, thanks, and honor to God, who is the reason for everything one has. No, midnight times are not easy times, but they are times which remind one that God is in charge and control, and that after the midnight comes the dawn, and that God is trustworthy, even in the midnight times. Today, if you find yourself in a midnight time, I encourage you not to look at the midnight but instead to look up to heaven and begin to pray to and praise the one who is able to change your midnight into dawn. My prayer for you today, if you are in a midnight time, is do not let your heart be troubled or your soul be in despair, but instead use the time to praise and trust in the Lord. Do you know that praise and trust keep the heart calm, the soul at peace, and the mind's focus off the midnight, while one waits for the dawn to come forth?

Footnote: Remember that when one is in the midnight times, the Lord is there also. If one will trust and depend on him, He will see one through the midnight and bring one safely into the dawn.

Trusting Him in Times of Trouble

Do not let your heart be troubled. Trust in God.
Also trust in me.

—John 14:1

You don't always know what to do or how to do it when it comes to life and the struggles and troubles of life. But the Lord knows what and how to take care of your life and your life's struggles and troubles if He is trusted to do so. Life in this world will bring times of trouble because in John 16:33 scripture, you read the words Jesus told His disciples, which reads, "In this world you will have trouble, but take heart for I have overcome the world." Here in this particular scripture, Jesus is forewarning His disciples about troubled times to come. He tells them to expect times of trouble so that when it happens, they would be able to have peace in Him. When it comes to times of trouble, it's not if it will but when. Trouble can strike at any time, through many ways and methods. Some trouble comes sometimes as a result of what you may have done, from others in your life, from the enemy, or even from God who uses troubled times for many reasons. For example, troubled times can be times of testing, training, and learning. Troubled times can also be a time to show those things hidden within the heart, such as unconfessed sins, unresolved issues, disbelief, doubt, and other things that are a hindrance to one moving forward in one's life instead of remaining in the same old way and position. Troubled times can be times of healing old hurts, heartaches, and wounds as well as times to build a stronger relationship with God and others. It's in times of trouble that growth and maturity develop, and it's in times of trouble one learns to depend on, rely on, and trust in God to meet the need, regardless of how the situation feels or looks. Trust is what keeps hope alive, faith strong, and doubt and discouragement out of the heart. Trust is one of the things we need in our lives because it is part of life's journey. Trust is necessary to get us through life's troubles, especially the troubles that hang around like a bad storm. As soon as it appears to be over, bingo, it's not. But sooner or later the trouble will clear out the same as the storm once it has run its course and accomplished what it came to do.

Some troubles come like a gentle breeze and then it's over. Others seem to linger and linger like a bad cold. Trouble is trouble, be it only for a brief moment or it lasts for a long time. It is still trouble, and God is still in the midst of it with you providing whatever He knows you need to survive. If it is strength, He strengthens, and if it is rest, He gives you rest. God gives you whatever you need to help you in your time of trouble. Ask, believe, and receive what you need in your time of trouble and He will supply. If you do the above three things in troubled times, God will certainly do it, if you only believe and trust Him to do so. In times of trouble, there are six things to believe and trust about God, and all of them begin with the letter *P*:

- First, believe and trust in his *presence*.
- Second, believe and trust in his *power*.
- Third, believe and trust in his *provision*.
- Fourth, believe and trust in his *protection*.
- Fifth, believe and trust in his *promises*.
- And sixth, believe and trust in his *peace*.

All six of these things you can believe and trust in God for in your time of trouble. You can have total confidence and comfort in God's love, compassion, and faithfulness in your time of trouble. No one wants trouble, but trouble wants everyone. We don't know when trouble may show up and show off or how long it may hang around when it comes, because only the Master knows such things about trouble. However, what you do know is that you won't ever be alone, for God will be there as well, and God is able to deal with any trouble you have. None of us know why we go through some of the trouble we go through, or even why if sometimes lasts for a long time. What you do know, however, is that God is with you and He knows what to do. Therefore, you have the assurance it will all work together for your good and His glory. To know this truth should encourage us to continue to stand firm in our faith, with your belief and trust in God to take care of you and the trouble in your life.

Footnote: No matter if you want it or not, you will have times of trouble. But you also will have with you God, who knows and understands what to do about the trouble. Therefore, let not your heart be troubled, but instead let your heart trust in God.

When God's in the Midst, Anything Can Happen

Now to him who is able to do immeasurably
more than all we ask or imagine, according to his
power that is at work within us.

—Ephesians 3:20

When God is in the midst of life's situations, your heart need not be troubled or fearful, for God is on your side, and He's in control. When God is in the midst of your life's troubles, they can become a time of triumph. When He is in the midst of your life's storms, they can become a time of success and sunshine. When God is in the midst of your life's problems, they can become a time of praise. Whatever your situation, God has the power to change what is into something totally different and opposite of what it is. With God, nothing is ever too hard or impossible for Him to do; you just have to believe and trust that He is able to turn things around for your good and His glory. Nothing is beyond God's knowledge or wisdom to accomplish. He can achieve anything. Everything is in His ability to do, if that is His will, plan, and purpose to do so. Life is full of situations, troubles, and challenges. There are many things that you face on life's journey. However, no obstacle that you face is too great to overcome when you put your faith, hope, confidence, and trust in God to help you in life's circumstances. No matter how hard or painful life's storms or situations can be on the journey, when you put your faith into the word, promises, and power of God, it helps you to have the confidence to be able to endure and overcome. When God is in the midst of your situations, look out, for anything can happen. God is not limited to what you think might happen or even the way you think it will.

God's thoughts and your thoughts are not the same, and neither is your way the same as God's way when it comes to doing things. Neither is His time or your time the same when it comes to a change over a matter that you have prayed about and wanted to be over or at least different than it continues to be. It's hard to deal with life and life's troubles, but the comfort to the soul on life's journey is in knowing that God is also on the journey and that He gives you, day by day, what is necessary to enable you to endure. When God is in the midst of life and life's problems, you can depend on Him to work the matter out. Even when there appears to be nothing happening, that is the time to start praising instead of complaining, worrying, and stressing for a breakthrough is on the horizon. When things are at their hardest, hope should be at its strongest, for a change is at hand, and sometimes that change is nearer and closer than you think. Oftentimes life's situations require a time of waiting. Waiting is hard when the wait is alone; but when faith, hope, expectation, anticipation, belief, and trust are added to the waiting period, it helps the soul to be encouraged, uplifted, and strengthened as he or she waits on the Lord. Sometimes the unexpected comes into one's life that wasn't part of one's plan, but nevertheless, it came to be. But even in one's unexpected times, it is wonderful to know that God knew about the unexpected and He already knows what to do. Therefore, you need not be anxious in heart when life brings forth a situation that you were not expecting, because God was, and He's able to take care of it.

Footnote: Remember that God is able to change what is into something totally different, if you trust Him to do so.

No Matter What, Don't Lose Heart

Do not let your heart be troubled, trust in God.

—John 14:1

No matter how dark, difficult, discouraging, or disappointing the situation is, no matter how hard, tough, or rough it becomes. No matter how challenging or painful it is to bear, no matter how unpleasant it is or how long the wait has been. No matter how impossible the matter looks, don't lose heart or hope; don't despair, don't give up and don't give in, no matter the situation, trouble, problem, or circumstance. For there's another chapter to the story and God is the writer. Therefore, hold on, for God is still with you, and He is still in control and in charge, and don't you forget.

Even though things remain and look the same, keep the faith, be strong, and have courage, for God is with you. He's on your side, and whatever you need to endure, He will supply—be it refuge, rest, strength, comfort, or help. Just hold on and don't lose heart, for there's another chapter to the story. Life's situations may begin in one way and end in another way. Life's darkest times can turn out to be the brightest, best, and most blessed of times. Troubles, trials, and tests will come forth, but the encouragement in such times is to know that God is with us. He is an ever-present help, which means we're never alone regardless of what comes forth.

The Lord is there through it all, reminding us that He loves us and He is able to help, but we must trust in Him no matter what and don't become discouraged, anxious, or fearful. But instead trust and do not let our hearts become troubled about what is happening. God has an ultimate purpose and plan for every situation. We might not understand the whys for many things in life, but we can trust that God is too wise, compassionate, and merciful to allow anything that is harmful and not helpful to come forth.

Everything happens at his appointed and set time, and He stays with us from the start to the finish. When He makes a promise, He is faithful to fulfill it. God can always be trusted, depended, and relied on; so don't lose heart or hope, for the story is not over because God has a different chapter than what is now to the story. His chapter always ends with "Wow, look at what God did, and only He could have done this!" Whatever your situation today may be, don't lose heart, but trust in the Lord, for the story is not yet over.

Footnote: The prescription for doubt is to have confidence that God will work it out.

He Cares about Your Storm

A furious squall came up, and the waves broke over the boat,
so that it was nearly swamped. Jesus was in the stern,
sleeping on a cushion. The disciples woke him and said,
"Teacher, don't you care if we drown?"

—Mark 4:37–38

We are never alone to face life's storms, because we always have a companion with us, and that companion is the Lord, who is with us as our supporter, encourager, counselor, comforter, guide, and helper. The Lord is there for us, no matter how rough or tough the storm becomes. We have a helper we can depend on and trust in to be present at all times. He wants us to feel His presence in the storm and to be confident, not only in His presence but also in His power and promises; and one of His promises is to be with us. It's the things one sometimes allows to enter into one's life in the midst of the storm, like worry and anxiousness, which can take a toll on one's emotions, which in turn can impact the way one acts and feels during the storm. The reality of life and life's journey is that there will be storms at times along the way. The journey does not always carry one through times of sunshine; sometimes there are times of storms. One does not know what awaits one during one's journey from one day to the next. One day could start off one way and end up another way. A storm can suddenly arise unexpectedly into one's life, such as a health issue; the death of a loved one, family member, or a close friend; or even a financial situation or the loss of a job. All can become storms and all could become overwhelming and difficult. Some storms can be a time of struggle and suffering. Some can be dark and last longer than others. Some can be tough, hard, and rough to endure, and some can test one's faith to the point of wanting to give up. God understands what some of our storms do to us, and He wants us to know that He is there with us in our storms. But we must have faith in Him more than the storm if we are to be able to withstand the storm, even though the storm is powerful and strong and even though the storm feels and looks like it is winning. God wants us to stand firm, steady, and steadfast in the faith and to focus on Him and His power to handle the storm in his time. No storm is greater or more powerful than God. Every storm has a season and a solution to it. Not only do life's storms have a season and a solution to come and end, there is also a reason, purpose, and plan for the storm. God knows every storm we will face, and He knows what to do about all. He is with you in your storm, and He is able to help you, if you trust the storm to Him and believe in your heart and soul that in due season and time the storm will end.

Although at times it may not feel or look so, it will end when it has served the purpose for its being. We do not walk by or react by what we feel but instead by faith, and we do not react by sight but again by faith. It is faith which allows the focus to be on God and not on the storm we are facing and going through. God is between you and your storm, and He cares even when it seems He is uninterested in you and your storm. Nothing could be further from the truth, because God cares deeply about you, your life, and your life's storms. Everything about you concerns Him, and that means your storms, from the biggest to the smallest, from the least to the greatest, all concern Him. But there are times and moments when one may wonder and think if God cares about what he or she is going through in the storm. No storm is the same and neither is the experience or results from the storm, and yet every storm God works out for our good and His glory. Even the storms we sometimes cause, or those we find ourselves in because of others situations or choices, God still uses them for our good and His glory. We may not know or understand the why or reason behind the storm, but we can have comfort and hope in knowing that God does, and that He is with us to help and

His grace is still sufficient, even in the darkest and most painful and hurtful storm. God cares, and He is present in the storm. However, it is fear, doubt, and frustration which prevent the soul from experiencing the presence of the Lord and the peace of the Lord. When it comes to the storms in one's life, one is called upon to keep his focus on the Lord instead of the storm. Focus on the storm weakens one's faith and impacts the way one reacts to and in the storm. Focus on God strengthens the soul, calms the heart, and protects the mind from negative thoughts. When it comes to the storms of life, God wants the focus to be on Him and not the storm, and He wants one to remember that He is also in the storm. Therefore, we need not to be afraid or fearful of the storm because He has control, power, and victory over the storm. When it is time, He will speak to the storm, and the storm shall be calm and quiet. Today, if there is a storm in your life, remember God is with you and He cares.

Footnote: God is with you in every storm, and He will bring you safely through them all.

Where Are You, God?

My God, My God, why have you forsaken me?
Why are you so far from saving me,
so far from the words of my groaning?

—Psalm 22:1–2

Have you ever found yourself overwhelmed, feeling uncertain and insecure about what to do over a certain matter? You have waited and waited, and all is the same. When things are not moving or proceeding as quickly as you would like, the questions sometimes asked are, "Where are you God? Don't you understand what is happening?" If you have found yourself asking or even thinking about these two questions, don't feel bad because you are not alone. These two questions have rolled out of the mouths of many like a bowling ball rolling down the aisle. Whether thought or spoken, these questions have been on the minds and hearts of many, especially in times of struggles and hard times. Often as we wait anxiously on the Lord's help, frustration and stress do not help the situation. They usually make it worse. Troubled times can certainly disturb and interrupt life. Troubled times can be a strain on the soul. And troubled times can have an impact on the way one thinks and acts. Sometimes the longer the trouble lasts, the greater the chance for the feelings of discouragement and dismay to grab hold of the heart.

Emotions from what the soul is experiencing can stir up certain feelings that cause the mind to think in a negative way about the situation. Sometimes, like David, one can feel forsaken, forgotten, and abandoned. However, the Lord, who is our Shepherd, is present.

He is ever-present in your life. It is one's feelings which help establish the foundation for the way one views and thinks about one's life and one's situations. What one thinks is what determines one's attitude and actions. Philippians 4:6–8 scripture suggests to do the following when it comes to a situation and thinking about that particular situation: First, it suggests that one be not anxious about anything. Second, the scripture suggests that one through prayer and petition, with a thankful heart, present one's request to God. And third, it suggests that one adjusts the way one thinks about one's troubles or problems. If one follows the suggestions from Philippians 4:6–8, I believe one will be able to control the way one feels and thinks about one's situation.

It becomes harder to sense and feel the presence of God if one's thoughts are negative toward God about one's situation. Negative thinking only produces a negative attitude, which leads to negative actions. A positive attitude allows the soul to remain at peace until God acts on what has been requested of him. When a request is asked of Him, it is good to remember that God acts by His time and not by your time. When it is considered that God operates on His time and in His way, this will help to keep the focus on God, His word, and His promises. When the mind is steadfast on God, one's emotions and feelings won't be able to convince one that God is not with one and that He is not concerned or cares about one's life or circumstance. The enemy and self can plant the seeds of distrust and doubt into the heart, if one is not careful about what one thinks and believes. Whatever one's situation is, it is important to guard one's mind and heart. Protect both the mind and heart by believing in God's power and trusting in his promise to always be there with one and to help one in times of trouble.

When souls are weary, weak, and worried, it is not hard for those souls in their unhealthy state to give birth to the triplets known as disbelief, distrust, and despair. All three of these are cousins to doubt and discouragement. None is a helper to the soul but instead a hindrance to the soul when it comes to that soul experiencing the presence and peace of God. Difficult times in life can become hard times, and hard times can become times of waiting, and times of waiting can bring forth at times the questions. Where are you, God, and, God, why have you forsaken me? Yes, there are moments when God is asked these questions. God understands the questions and why they are asked. But He also hopes that His answer will give comfort and peace, which is, "I will never leave or forsake you, for I am ever-present."

Footnote: Remember that God is with you in every situation. He promised to always be with you, and He never breaks a promise.

He's Been There for Me, as Promised

I will never leave you, nor forsake you.

—Hebrews 13:5

I held on to His promise, never to leave me, never to forsake me; and He has demonstrated countless times in my life to be faithful, trustful, and dependable to His promise. He has been there for me as promised. Never once in my time of need, and there have been many, has He ever waivered on his promise. He has always been there for me, taking care of me, leading me, guiding me, comforting me, encouraging me, strengthening me, and pointing me in the right direction. He has been there for me when I needed a friend and no one was in sight. He has supported me in my suffering. There has never been a moment when He has not been available for me to look up to the heavens and call on Him for help. Through every trial I've gone through, trouble or problems I have been faced with, He has always, always been there for me. My burdens He carried; in my time of sorrow and weeping, He comforted me. He has always been right there to carry me through. In my time of weakness, He has been there to strengthen me, help me, and uphold me with His righteous right hand. He has literally always been there for me time and time again.

In my times of distress, He has uplifted my soul and spirit with the following words: "I am with you forever. I will never leave you nor forsake you. I am with you. Be strong and of good courage. Stand firm in your faith. You are not alone. I am here with you. Never will I leave you nor forsake you. I am with you forever. Regardless of how it looks right now, I am with you. Be encouraged, I will never leave you nor forsake you. I am with you forever. Remain faithful. Don't lose hope, don't be discouraged, and don't give up. I am here for you. Trust in me. Depend on me and rely on me. I have not abandoned you. Have confidence; you belong to me. I will take care of you. Be patient. Be obedient. I am with you forever. Be content. Be joyful. I chose you, and now you belong to me. I am here for you. I care for you. I am with you. Nothing will separate you from me. I am with you forever, forever and forever. I will be with you even to the end of time. Wait on me, I will never leave you nor forsake you. I am here for you. I love you. I am with you forever and forever. Don't lose hope and don't give up. Keep pressing on, be strong, and be of good courage. Stand firm in your faith. I am with you now and forever. Even to the end of time, I will be with you." Therefore, I can say with trust and confidence that He will always be there for me as promised. He will never leave me nor forsake me. He is always there for me as promised, no matter what.

Footnote: God has always been there for me as promised, and you can trust Him to always be there for you, no matter what.

The Voice

Be still and know that I am God.

—Psalm 46:10

There is a voice which speaks the words, "Be still and know that I am God." It is a voice reminding you that God is always with you. It is a voice inviting one to trust one's situations and troubles to God who is able and powerful enough to do anything. It is a voice deep within; a voice of calmness. It is a voice calling gently, softly, and slowly to the hurting; a voice uplifting to the mind. It is a voice comforting to the heart; a voice soothing to the soul. There is a voice full of compassion, care, and concern. It is a voice speaking out to the wounded, broken, and hopeless; a voice to the fearful, fretful, and frustrated. There is a voice with healing power; a voice reaching out to the dismayed, depressed, and desperate. It is a voice embracing the sorrowful and grieving; a voice truthful and trustworthy.

There is a voice seeking the lost and sin sick. It is a voice encouraging the troubled and suffering not to give up, no matter what the situation looks or feels like; a voice which strengthens the weak in times of hardship. There is a voice which offers support and refuge to the weary and restless. It is a voice of wisdom and knowledge to help the uncertain, unsure, and undecided. There is a voice of confidence. It is a voice of authority; a voice of power. There is a voice seasoned with grace, mercy, and faithfulness. It is a voice of kindness; a voice of quietness. It is a voice of love; a voice of stillness. It is the voice of

Him who says, "Be still and know that I am God, and I am always there for you."

Footnote: There is a voice that speaks the words, "Be still and know that I am God." The question is, are you listening?

He's with You Always

And surely I am with you always,
to the very end of the age.

—Matthew 28:20

These are powerful words meant to touch the soul in a deep and profound way. Jesus in this verse was giving the disciples the assurance that He would be there for them, regardless. Their footprints would be his footprints. Everywhere they walked, so would He. Whatever they faced, so would He. When life's journey became hard, He would be there to help them through. In other words, Jesus was reminding them that He would always be with them. These words Jesus spoke to the disciples would be words to comfort and strengthen the soul in troubled times. These same words—I am with you always—are still words to comfort and encourage souls today. God is always with you; He is constantly there for you. Wherever you go or whatever you face, the Lord will be with you. He will be there to provide and protect you. You never need to be afraid or fearful no matter what, for God is with you and He will help you. He will support and strengthen you. He will never ever leave you alone. He will be right by your side, encouraging you to be strong and courageous and reminding you that His grace is always sufficient.

As you go through life's journey, you may just discover that God is present and He works out every single one of your troubles for your good and His glory. You even may discover that He is able to do what is viewed as the impossible. And you also may discover He is faithful and trustworthy. Sometimes your situation may be somewhat less favorable. However, the good news is that God is still in control and He is also with you. God will never leave you in difficult and demanding times. No matter the trouble or tests you face, He is there to offer his support. And his support and help is something you can take to heart with full confidence. God does not say He will do something and not be able to follow through on what He said. You can always count and depend on God to act on whatever He said and promised. Whatever situation you find yourself in, remember that God is there for you, even when it seems like He is not.

In all of your troubles or trials in life, you can count on God to be there for you. God is ever-present. He's there for you, surrounding you with His love and peace in life's trying times. The God of compassion and comfort is there in all of your life's situations. He will not leave you alone; God is there at all times, from the easy times to the difficult times. He will be there to bring peace to the soul and comfort to the heart in such times. Wherever you go or whatever you face, remember God cares about you and will never leave or forsake you. You need not wonder or question if God is with you, for He is. You can have complete confidence in this assurance. Jesus told His disciples that they needed not to worry about being alone to face any trouble, for He would be there to face it with them. That same Jesus who spoke the words, "I am with you always," to the disciples in Matthew 28:20 is also with us in our troubles.

Footnote: We are never alone, for Jesus is always with us. The words of Jesus should cause us to rejoice.

About the Author

I rene Bryan was born in Williamston, North Carolina, and raised in Bassett, Virginia. She holds a Bachelor of Arts degree in sociology from the University of Maryland and a diploma from the Institute of Children's Literature. She has also completed a number of correspondence courses in theology from Andersen University, Indiana. In addition, she has taught in various schools on military installations both stateside and overseas during her husband's military career. Irene is an ordained minister in the Church of God and so is her husband Rodney. Irene and Rodney have one daughter named Tanya. Irene enjoys doing crafts, crocheting, and cooking. She also enjoys encouraging, inspiring, and helping people; and she especially enjoys doing inspirational writing.

CPSIA information can be obtained
at www.ICGtesting.com
Printed in the USA
LVHW110345030221
678219LV00006B/613